Utilitarian Ethics and the Psychopath

Biblical and Scientific Perspectives on Moral Evil

Dr. Timothy Gordon

Author's Preface

This short monograph on the utilitarian ethics of psychopaths is a forensic and biblical case study of the problem of moral evil. The purpose of this study was to look at what I call an objective or real-world perspective on what moral evil looks like. In this study I was not interested in rehashing the same theological and philosophical arguments on evil because there are many other resources that do that. The attempt here is to show that moral evil exists because there are individuals who exist who are truly evil by their nature. An additional purpose is to show that psychopaths demonstrate a type of utilitarian ethic known as ethical egoism. This study is not exhaustive by any means but is designed to make the reader literate about what moral evil looks like in this one case study on psychopaths. Future studies will choose other examples such as those who murder and destroy in the name of a religion or other worldview.

Blessings,

Tim Gordon
Boise, Idaho

Table of Contents

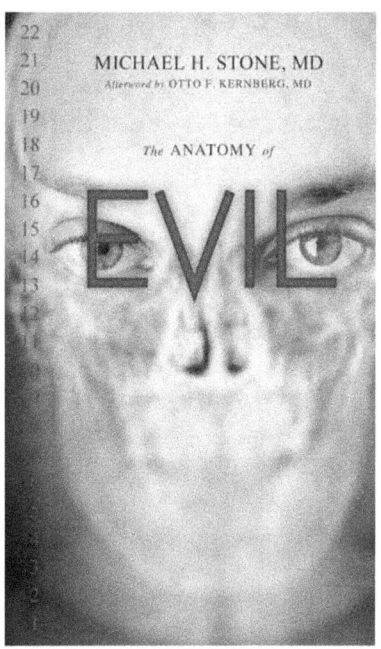

THESIS

This monograph within the framework of biblical and scientific perspectives on moral evil examines the clinical, forensic, and biblical perspectives of psychopaths and the system of ethics they use. I will define the main terms of the study and provide brief overviews of the history of psychopathy and psychopathic traits and characteristics. I will review how psychopaths are diagnosed and look at some statistics on psychopathy. The study will focus on the ethics and science of psychopathy. The appendices include some extra material on case studies, Ezekiel 18, and Dr. Stone's Gradations of Evil Scale. Finally, I am not a clinical or technical expert in the field of psychopathy or forensic psychology. My expertise is in the area of Christian apologetics where I have done doctoral research on the problem of evil and specifically, for this study, the ethics of psychopaths and the possible correlations of the clinical and forensic perspectives on evil with the biblical perspectives.

RESEARCH QUESTIONS

1. What are the distinctions between the psychopathy, sociopathy, and antisocial personality disorder (APD)?

2. What ethical theories are relevant to a study of psychopathy?

3. What is the historical development of psychopathy?

4. What are the clinical traits and characteristics of psychopaths?

5. Who are some notable psychopaths of history and the Bible?

6. How are psychopaths diagnosed?

7. What are some statistics on psychopathy?

8. What are some clinical and forensic perspectives on the ethics of psychopathy?

9. What are some clinical and forensic perspectives on evil?

10. What are some biblical perspectives on evil?

DEFINITIONS: PSYCHOPATHY AND SOCIOPATHY

Psychopathy: A personality disorder described by the personality traits and behaviors that form the basis of this book. Psychopaths are without conscience and incapable of empathy, guilt, or loyalty to anyone but themselves.

Sociopathy: Not a formal psychiatric condition. It refers to patterns of attitudes and behaviors that are considered antisocial and criminal by society at large but are seen as normal or necessary by the subculture or social environment in which they developed. Sociopaths may have a well-developed conscience and a normal capacity for empathy, guilt, and loyalty, but their sense of right and wrong is based on the norms and expectations of their subculture or group. Many criminals might be described as sociopaths (Hare and Babiak, SiS, 19).

DEFINITIONS: ANTISOCIAL PERSONALITY DISORDER

A broad diagnostic category found in the APA's DSM-IV. Antisocial and criminal behaviors play a major role in its definition and, in this sense, APD is similar to sociopathy. Some of those with APD are psychopaths, but many are not.

The difference between psychopathy and antisocial personality disorder is that the former includes personality traits such as lack of empathy, grandiosity, and shallow emotion that are not necessary for a diagnosis of APD. APD is three or four times more common than psychopathy in the general population and in prisons. The prevalence of those we would describe as sociopathic is unknown but likely is considerably higher than that of APD (Hare and Babiak, SiS, 19).

DEFINITIONS: UTILITARIAN ETHICS

The view that the morally right action is the action that produces the most good. There are many ways to spell out this general claim. Utilitarianism is a form of consequentialism: the right action is understood entirely in terms of consequences produced. What distinguishes utilitarianism from egoism has to do with the scope of the relevant consequences. On the utilitarian view one ought to maximize the overall good — that is, consider the good of others as well as one's own good. The classical utilitarians, Jeremy Bentham and John Stuart Mill, identified the good with pleasure, so, like Epicurus, were hedonists about value. They also held that we ought to maximize the good, that is, bring about 'the greatest amount of good for the greatest number" (Fedler, *ECE*).

DEFINITIONS: CONSEQUENTIALISM

The ends justify the means. Consequentialists contend that actions are to be judged not by some inherent quality but by the consequences that they produce. The main type of consequentialism is called utilitarianism. The most important early proponents of utilitarianism were Jeremy Bentham (1748-1832) and John Stuart Mill (1806-1873). So when deciding between two courses of action, one must perform the action that will result in the greatest amount of good for the greatest number of people. The action that has the greatest overall "utility" (proportion of good consequences to bad) is the right action. What makes an action right or wrong are the consequences of the action (Fedler, *ECE*, 426-431).

DEFINITIONS: ETHICAL EGOISM

This is the mode of ethical reasoning behind the oft-repeated phrase "Look out for number one." This mode of reasoning simply asks the question, "What is best for me?" It is understood as a consequentialist theory in which the consequences for the individual agent are taken to matter more than any other result. It says that decisions should he based on the following principle: Everyone should act so as to maximize his or her own benefit. Jesus explicitly rejects ethical egoism by calling on his followers to place the needs of others above their own: "Whoever wants to be first must he last of all and servant of all" (Mark 9:35) (Fedler, *ECE*, 224-233).

DEFINITIONS: MORAL EVIL

This is sin, disorder in the moral world. It is the failure of rational and free beings to conform in character and conduct to the will of God. This is the greatest evil (see Rom 1:18-32).

Figure 1 - 9/11 Terrorist Attack

How the existence of evil is compatible with the goodness of God is the question of theodicy. Recent examples include the terrorist attack of 9/11, the Holocaust, and personal crimes committed against others as illustrated in Figures 1-3.

Figure 2 - Nazi Holocaust Against the Jews

In Luke 13:2 Jesus speaks of Pilate killing some Galileans while they were offering sacrifices. Source: Gordon, Know What You Believe.

Figure 3 - Kermit Smith, Jr, Murderer

HISTORY OF PSYCHOPATHY

Condition first described clinically in 1801, by the French surgeon Philippe Pinel. He called it "mania without delirium."

In early 19th century, American surgeon Benjamin Rush wrote about a type of "moral derangement" in which the sufferer was neither delusional nor psychotic but nevertheless engaged in profoundly antisocial behavior, including horrifying acts of violence. Rush noted that the condition appeared early in life.

The term "moral insanity" became popular in the mid-nineteenth century and was widely used in the U.S. and in England to describe incorrigible criminals.

The word "psychopath" (literally, "suffering soul") was coined in Germany in the 1880s.

By the 1920s, "constitutional psychopathic inferiority" had become the catchall phrase psychiatrists used for a general mixture of violent and antisocial characteristics found in irredeemable criminals, who appeared to lack a conscience.

In the late 1930s, an American psychiatrist named Hervey Cleckley began collecting data on a certain kind of patient he encountered in the course of his work in a psychiatric hospital in Augusta, Georgia.

Cleckley isolated 16 traits exhibited by patients he called "primary" psychopaths; these included being charming and intelligent, unreliable, dishonest, irresponsible, self-centered, emotionally shallow, and lacking in empathy and insight.

Cleckley eventually wrote what has become a classic textbook on psychopathy, *The Mask of Sanity*. Originally published in 1941, this definitive book is now in its 5th edition (1976) and was one of the first books to present a clear picture of psychopathy.

The psychiatric profession wanted little to do with psychopathy, because it was thought to be incurable.

The emphasis in the word "psychopath" on an internal sickness was at odds with liberal mid-century social thought, which tended to look for external causes of social deviancy; "sociopath," coined in 1930 by the psychologist G. E. Partridge, became the preferred term.

In 1958, the American Psychiatric Association (APA) used the term "sociopathic personality" to describe the disorder in its Diagnostic and Statistical Manual of Mental Disorders (DSM).

In the 1968 edition, the condition was renamed "general antisocial personality disorder (ASPD)."

In the early 1960s Robert Hare began a 25-year study of psychopathy that would be his life's work. Today Hare is considered the top authority in the world on psychopathy and the Hare Psychopathy Checklist (PCL) that he developed is the only valid instrument used to diagnose psychopathy.

In the last decade Kent Kiehl has begun using a mobile MRI unit (fMRI) to scan the brains of psychopaths in New Mexico to determine if there are biological markers for psychopathy. The research reveals that the brains of psychopaths are different than normal human brains in the paralimbic region. At the same time, molecular biologists are analyzing DNA to try and identify possible genetic markers (Seabrook, "Suffering Souls", *New Yorker*).

PIONEERS IN PSYCHOPATHY

Dr. Hervey Cleckley   Dr. Robert Hare

DIAGNOSING PSYCHOPATHS

The Hare Psychopathy Checklist-Revised (PCL-R) is a diagnostic tool used to rate a person's psychopathic or antisocial tendencies. Originally designed for forensic use, the PCL-R consists of a 20-item symptom rating scale that allows qualified examiners to compare a subject's degree of psychopathy with that of a prototypical psychopath.

The PCL-R is published by Multi-Health Systems (MHS), as are its derivatives, the PCL:SV, The APSD, and the P-Scan. There are 20 items scored from interview & file data. Each item is scored on a 3-point scale. The total score 0-40; extent to which an individual matches prototypical psychopath.

The PCL-R was developed for forensic use, but now used in a variety of contexts. It was originally developed for adults, but new scales established for adolescents (PCL:YV). Psychopathy research is discussed based on PCL-R or its derivatives.

The PCL-R is accepted by many in the field as the best method for determining the presence and extent of psychopathy in a person. The PCL-R is still used to diagnose members of the original population for which it was developed—adult males in prisons, criminal psychiatric hospitals, and awaiting psychiatric evaluations or trial in other correctional and detention facilities. Recent experience suggests that the PCL-R may also be used effectively to diagnose sex offenders as well as female and adolescent offenders (Hare, Without Conscience: Understanding and Treating Psychopaths, Handout; EMD, Mind Disorders).

PSYCHOPATHIC TRAITS AND CHARACTERISTICS

Interpersonal	Affective	Lifestyle	Antisocial
Glib and superficial charm	Lack of remorse/guilt	Stimulation seeking	Poor behavior controls
Grandiose sense of self-worth	Shallow affect	Impulsivity	Early behavior problems
Pathological lying	Callous lack of empathy	Irresponsible	Juvenile delinquency
Conning and manipulation	Failure to accept responsibility	Parasitic lifestyle	Revocation of conditional release
		Lack of realistic goals	Criminal versatility

Robert D. Hare, Hare Psychopathy Checklist-Revised, 2nd ed. (Toronto, ON: Multi-Health Systems, 2003).

PSYCHOPATHY STATISTICS

The cause of psychopathy is unknown. On average, about 20 percent of male and female prison inmates are psychopaths. Psychopaths are responsible for more than 50 percent of the serious crimes committed (Hare, *WC*, 87). The recidivism rate of psychopaths is about double that of other offenders. The violent recidivism rate of psychopaths is about triple that of other offenders (Hare, *WC*, 96).

A recent study by the FBI found that 44% of the offenders who killed a law enforcement officer on duty were psychopaths (Hare, *WC*, 87). Serial killers are extremely rare; probably fewer than 100 in North America. There may be as many as 3-4 million psychopaths in North America or about 1 in every 100 in the general population (Hare, *WC*, 74). On average, the criminal activities of psychopaths remain at a high level until around age forty, after which they decrease sharply (Hare, *WC*, 97).

SUBCRIMINAL (WHITE COLLAR) PSYCHOPATHS

Many psychopaths never go to prison or any other facility. They appear to function reasonably well — as lawyers, doctors, psychiatrists, academics, mercenaries, police officers, cult leaders, military personnel, businesspeople, writers, artists, entertainers, and so forth — without breaking the law, or at least without being caught and convicted.

These individuals are every bit as egocentric, callous, and manipulative as the average criminal psychopath; however, their intelligence, family background, social skills, and circumstances permit them to construct a facade of normalcy and to get what they want with relative impunity. Their conduct, although technically not illegal, typically violates conventional ethical standards, hovering just on the shady side of the law.

Unlike people who consciously adopt a ruthless, greedy, and apparently unscrupulous strategy in their business dealings but who are reasonably honest and empathetic in other areas of their lives, subcriminal psychopaths exhibit much the same behaviors and attitudes in all areas of their lives. If they lie and cheat on the job—and get away with it or are even admired for it—they will lie and cheat in other areas of their lives (Hare, *WC*, 113-114).

NOTABLE PSYCHOPATHS OF RECENT HISTORY

John Wayne Gacy, a Des Plaines, Illinois, contractor and Junior Chamber of Commerce "Man of the Year" who entertained children as "Pogo the Clown," had his picture taken with President Carter's wife, Rosalynn, and murdered thirty-two young men in the 1970s, burying most of the bodies in the crawl space under his house. Convicted of 33 murders, Gacy was sentenced to death for 12 of these killings on March 13, 1980. He spent 14 years on death row before he was executed by lethal injection at Stateville Correctional Center on May 10, 1994 (Hare, WC, 3).

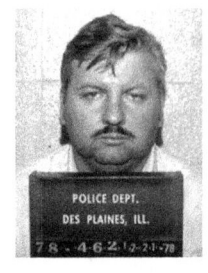

Scott Lee Peterson (born October 24, 1972) is a man convicted of murdering his wife, Laci Peterson, and their unborn son in Modesto, California in 2002. Peterson's arrest and subsequent trial received significant American news media coverage until 2005, when he was sentenced to death by lethal injection. He remains on death row in San Quentin State Prison while his case is on appeal to the Supreme Court of California. He maintains his innocence. Many trial watchers came to see Scott Peterson as a manipulative, charming, pathological liar with a grandiose sense of self and an inability to empathize (Hare and Babiak,

SIS, 66).

Ted Bundy, was an American serial killer, rapist, kidnapper, and necrophile who assaulted and murdered numerous young women and girls during the 1970s and possibly earlier. After more than a decade of denials, he confessed shortly before his execution to 30 homicides committed in seven states between 1974 and 1978; the true total remains unknown and could be much higher. Bundy died in the electric chair at Raiford Prison in Starke, Florida, on January 24, 1989 (Wikipedia).

Aileen Carol Wuornos was a serial killer who killed seven men in Florida in 1989 and 1990. Wuornos claimed that her victims had either raped or attempted to rape her while she was working as a prostitute, and that all of the homicides were committed in self-defense. She was convicted and sentenced to death for six of the murders and was executed by the State of Florida by lethal injection on October 9, 2002. She scored a 32 on the PCL-R. Wuornos was arguably one of only two women cases worldwide in the last century of women who independently committed serial sexual murder. In 2003 Charlize Theron won the Academy Best Actress award for her portrayal of Wuornos in the film Monster (Myers, Gooch, Meloy, 1).

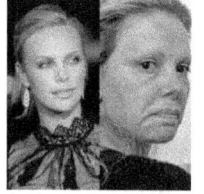

Cain. In the biblical narrative of Genesis 4:1-16, Cain murdered his brother Abel in a jealous rage, lied about the murder to God, and as a result was cursed and marked for life.[5] With the earth left cursed to drink Abel's blood, Cain was no longer able to farm the land. Cain was punished as a "fugitive and wanderer." Verse 8 seems to clearly indicate Cain's murder of Abel was premeditated. He deliberately lied to the LORD when questioned about Abel's whereabouts. His reply is cold and callous, without empathy in verse 9. The apostle John wrote, "We should not be like Cain, who was of the evil one and murdered his brother. And why did he murder him? Because his own deeds were evil and his brother's righteous."

Amenhotep II was likely the pharaoh of the Exodus in 1446 BC. He placed the Israelites in hard bondage, made them make bricks without straw, and opposed Moses and Aaron. He showed no concern for his country or people when Egypt was decimated by the 10 plagues. His heart was hardened. He pretended to repent until the plague was removed and then hardened his heart again. His army chased Israel and was destroyed in the Red Sea (Ex. 5-15).

Jezebel was a Sidonian princess and Baal worshipper. It was a regular practice of Baal worship to sacrifice children in the fire. She also murdered the prophets of the LORD. She married Israelite king Ahab and incited his idol worship. She coldly and callously had Naboth killed when he would not sell his vineyard to Ahab. She came to a violent end when she was thrown out the window and eaten by dogs (I Kings 16-21; II Kings 9).

Herod the Great was the Edomite ruler of the Jews from 37-4 BC. He has been described as "a madman who murdered his own family and a great many rabbis", "the evil genius of the Judean nation", "prepared to commit any crime in order to gratify his unbounded ambition" and "the greatest builder in Jewish history". He murdered his wife and two of his sons. When he heard about the birth of Jesus, he ordered all of the male children 2 years old and under in Bethlehem to be killed. Matthew 2:16-18 records this atrocity prophesied by Jeremiah.

THE PSYCHOPATHIC STARE

Many psychopaths tend to have a distinctive stare as if they are staring right through you. The psychopath's fixated, intense stare is sometimes referred to as *scoptophlia*: the sexualization of looking; predatory staring. It is visual predation (Birch, "Psychopathy: Is It In Their Eyes?" *Psychopaths & Love*).

Dr. Robert Hare says, "It's their eyes that are the most remarkable feature. How they drill into you." (Seabrook, "Suffering Souls", *New Yorker*.). It tends to be penetrating, emotionless, expressionless or they may have an evil smirk. The kind of stare that gives you the willies.

Many people find it difficult to deal with the intense, emotionless, or "predatory" stare of the psychopath...the fixated stare of the psychopath is more a prelude to self-gratification and the exercise of power than simple interest or empathic caring (Hare, *WC*, 208).

The Ethics of Psychopathy

Unlike psychotic individuals, psychopaths are rational and aware of what they are doing and why. Their behavior is the result of choice, freely exercised (Hare, *WC*, 22).

Psychopaths are generally more willing than non-psychopaths to endorse impersonal harms or rule violations in order to achieve certain beneficial outcomes. If challenged or caught in a lie, psychopaths are not embarrassed. They simply change or elaborate on the story line to weave together all the misarranged details into a believable fabric (Babiak and Hare,

SIS, 50).

Another characteristic of psychopaths is an ability to avoid taking responsibility for things that go wrong; instead, they blame others, circumstances, fate, and so forth. As it does in the assessment phase, lack of empathy, guilt, or remorse plays an important role during the manipulation phase — by facilitating behavior that is callous and insensitive to the rights and feeling of others (Babiak and Hare, *SIS*, 51-52).

Irresponsibility, another one of the twenty traits that Hare uses to define the psychopath, is not an unusual trait (Babiak and Hare, *SIS*, 56). Lying, deceiving, and manipulation are natural talents for psychopaths (Hare, *WC*, 46).

Psychopaths show a stunning lack of concern for the devastating effects their actions have on others. Often, they are completely forthright about the matter, calmly stating that they have no sense of guilt, are not sorry for the pain and destruction they have caused, and that there is no reason for them to be concerned (Hare, *WC*, 40-41).

Psychopaths view people as little more than objects to be used for their own gratification. The weak and the vulnerable — whom they mock, rather than pity — are favorite. Psychopaths display a general lack of empathy. They are indifferent to the rights and suffering of family members and strangers alike. If they do maintain ties with their spouses or children it is only because they see their family members as possessions, much like their stereos or automobiles (Hare, *WC*, 44-45).

This indifference to the welfare of children — their own as well as those of the man or woman they happen to be living with at the time — is a common theme in our files of psychopaths (Hare, *WC*, 63).

Most psychopaths begin to exhibit serious behavioral problems at an early age. These might include persistent lying, cheating, theft, fire setting, truancy, class disruption, substance abuse, vandalism, violence, bullying, running away, and precocious sexuality. Early cruelty to animals is usually a sign of serious emotional or behavioral problems (Hare, WC, 66).

The media frequently reports that witnesses and neighbors are taken completely by surprise in reaction to some senseless crime: "I just can't believe he was capable of doing a thing like that— there was absolutely no hint that he would do it." Adam Lanza who murdered the 20 children in Connecticut is a recent example. Reactions of this sort reflect not only psychopaths' power to manipulate others' impressions of themselves but the witnesses' ignorance of their early history (Hare, WC, 67).

Psychopaths have little aptitude for experiencing the emotional responses—fear and anxiety—that are the mainsprings of conscience. The psychopath carries out his evaluation of a situation— what he will get out of it and at what cost— without the usual anxieties, doubts, and concerns about being humiliated, causing pain, sabotaging future plans, in short, the infinite possibilities that people of conscience consider when deliberating possible actions (Hare, WC, 76, 78).

Unlike most other criminals, psychopaths show no loyalty to groups, codes, or principles, other than to "look out for number one." (Hare, WC, 85).

In one important study of utilitarian moral judgment of psychopaths, the main hypothesis that low-anxious psychopaths, but not high-anxious psychopaths, would endorse a significantly greater proportion of the personal moral actions than would the non-psychopaths was confirmed by the prediction (M. Koenigs, SCAN, 710).

THE SCIENCE OF PSYCHOPATHY

Recent studies on psychopaths utilize utilitarian moral dilemmas to assess their moral capabilities. A recent study by Spanish researchers used functional magnetic resonance imaging (fMRI) to prove that alterations in the brain network subserving moral judgment in criminal psychopaths are not limited to the inadequate network use during moral judgment, but that a primary network breakdown would exist with dysfunctional alterations outside moral dilemma situations. The alterations reported herein, may directly relate to one of the main behavioral traits of psychopaths, such as the inappropriate assembling of knowledge and action when offending people (J. Pujol, et. al, SCAN, 917, 922).

Another study by three researchers tested a prominent view of psychopathic moral reasoning suggesting that psychopathic individuals cannot properly distinguish between moral wrongs and other types of wrongs. The present study evaluated this view by examining the extent to which 109 incarcerated offenders with varying degrees of psychopathy could distinguish between moral and conventional transgressions relative to each other and to non-incarcerated healthy controls. The authors concluded that, contrary to earlier claims, insufficient data exist to infer that psychopathic individuals cannot know what is morally wrong (Aharoni, Sinnot-Armstrong, Kiehl, 1).

In a recent study, American researchers tested a dual-process theory synthesizing intuitive and emotional processes. Their theory associates utilitarian moral judgment (approving of harmful actions that maximize good consequences) with controlled cognitive processes and associates non-utilitarian moral judgment with automatic emotional responses. They concluded that, consistent with their theory, a cognitive load manipulation selectively interferes with utilitarian judgment. This interference effect provides direct evidence for the influence of controlled cognitive processes in moral judgment, and utilitarian moral judgment more specifically (J. Green, et. al, Cognitive Load Selectively Interferes with Utilitarian Moral Judgment, 1).

Another study of central interest is whether emotions play a causal role in moral judgment, and, in parallel, how emotion-related areas of the brain contribute to moral judgment. The study of 6 patients with focal bilateral damage to the ventromedial prefrontal cortex (VMPC), a brain region necessary for the normal generation of emotions and, in particular, social emotions, produced an abnormally 'utilitarian' pattern of judgments on moral dilemmas that pit compelling considerations of aggregate welfare against highly emotionally aversive behaviors (for example, having to sacrifice one person's life to save a number of other lives). In contrast, the VMPC patients' judgments were normal in other classes of moral dilemmas. These findings indicate that, for a selective set of moral dilemmas, the VMPC is critical for normal judgments of right and wrong. The findings support a necessary role for emotion in the generation of those judgments (M. Koenigs, et. al. Damage to the prefrontal cortex increases utilitarian moral judgments, 1).

In another study subject psychopaths were presented with a set of moral dilemmas. The researchers concluded that psychopaths make the same kind of moral distinctions as healthy individuals when it comes to evaluating the permissibility of an action embedded in a moral dilemma. These results force a rejection of the strong hypothesis that emotional processes are causally necessary for judgments of moral dilemmas, suggesting instead that psychopaths understand the distinction between right and wrong, but do not care about such knowledge, or the consequences that ensue from their morally inappropriate behavior (Cima, et. al, 59, 66).

In a study testing whether antisocial personality traits predict utilitarian responses, researchers gave participants a set of moral dilemmas widely used by behavioral scientists who study morality, like the following: "A runaway trolley is about to run over and kill five people, and you are standing on a footbridge next to a large stranger; your body is too light to stop the train, but if you push the stranger onto the tracks, killing

him, you will save the five people. Would you push the man?"

The authors concluded the study does not resolve the ethical debate, but it points to a flaw in the widely-adopted use of sacrificial dilemmas to identify optimal moral judgment. These methods fail to distinguish between people who endorse utilitarian moral choices because of underlying emotional deficits (like those captured by our measures of psychopathy and Machiavellianism) and those who endorse them out of genuine concern for the welfare of others." (Bartels and Pizarro, Antisocial Personality Traits Predict Utilitarian Responses to Moral Dilemmas, *Science Daily*).

THE SCIENCE OF EVIL

...when science holds the magnifying glass to evil, it is looking at the same set of motives that apply to bad actions in general: actions motivated by the usual suspects of jealousy, greed, lust, revenge, hatred, and the desire to avoid public humiliation. There will be no key that opens all doors to the mystery of evil: no "evil gene," no specific type of parental brutality that underlies all cases we label evil and that can be understood as a causative factor guaranteed to produce evil. Instead, we will see only a complex menu of "risk factors": a vegetable soup, if you will, of factors from which, if the soup simmers long enough, and if some of the special ingredients we listed above are mixed in, evil may eventually rise to the surface (Stone, TAE, 3656-3661).

CLINICAL DEFINITION OF EVIL

Evil applies only to human beings. Evil is reserved for describing certain acts done by people who clearly intended to hurt or to kill others in an excruciatingly painful way. Another requirement for using the term evil is that the perpetrator be aware that the victim would suffer intensely, experience agony-the same as the perpetrator knows he would feel if the tables were turned and he were the victim of those same actions

(Stone, *TAE*, 158-162).

For an act to reach the level of evil-whether violent or murderous or simply humiliating or sadistic in the extreme, though without violence-an intense narcissism is almost always part of the personality makeup: the red thread that runs through all the persons we have encountered earlier. This characteristic stands out unmistakably, for example, in the men who "stage" the murders of their wives, hoping to make the murder appear as an accident or as the act of some other assailant (Stone, *TAE*, 3626-3628).

Being male or female makes a big difference: males are far more likely to commit violent, including "evil," acts. Gender is something we inherit, but once we start out in life as a male or a female, expectations and experiences begin to differ-to a significant degree because of the sex we were born into (Stone, *TAE*, 3633-3634).

Three personality disorders have a close relationship to crime, particularly to violent crime. The evil actions described here are often the by-products of these disorders, whether singly or in combination. The three disorders are antisocial, psychopathic, and sadistic. A fourth-schizoid-deserves consideration as well because schizoid personality is seen in about half of the men committing serial sexual homicide (Stone, *TAE*, 4023-4025).

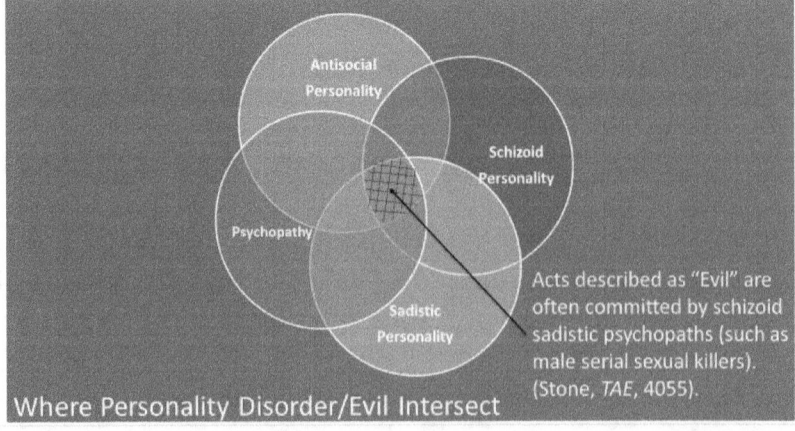

Acts described as "Evil" are often committed by schizoid sadistic psychopaths (such as male serial sexual killers). (Stone, *TAE*, 4055).

Where Personality Disorder/Evil Intersect

If we wanted to narrow our focus to single out the personality configuration that is connected with particular closeness to our concept of evil, it would be at the place where psychopathy, sadistic personality, and schizoid/autistic-spectrum disorders all come together (Stone, *TAE*, 4049-4050).

BIBLICAL PERSPECTIVES ON EVIL

Evil exists as an inexplicable, irrational force in the world. This is why it is important to continue thinking about evil in terms of a person. To do so keeps us from explaining evil simply as a weakness of will or knowledge. Thinking about evil in personal terms also keeps us vigilant about the sin and evil in our own lives. It helps us to keep watch for it lurking at our door or hiding in some unexpected form (Fedler, *ECE*, 1238-1241).

To end evil God would have to destroy the cause of evil – people. In His good plan for people, it is therefore not good to end all evil immediately. To do that, God would have to take away our ability to choose. But choice – free will – is a good thing. In order to love, you must be able to choose to love. Forced love is not love. So to have a universe that included love, God had to make us with choice, which includes the choice not to love – and that makes sin, evil, pain and suffering possible.

The person committing evil does not want God to stop their evil acts. They just think it would be good if God stopped certain evil acts or just the evil acts of others. But that would make life impossible. There would be no freedoms, no regularity and no personal responsibility.

BIBLE SCRIPTURES ON MORAL EVIL

The LORD saw that the wickedness of man was great in the earth, and that every intention of the thoughts of his heart was only evil continually (ESV Genesis 6:5).

And when the LORD smelled the pleasing aroma, the LORD said in his heart, "I will never again curse the ground because of man, for the intention of man's heart is evil from his youth (ESV Genesis 8:21).

We have all become like one who is unclean, and all our righteous deeds are like a polluted garment. We all fade like a leaf, and our iniquities, like the wind, take us away. There is no one who calls upon your name, who rouses himself to take hold of you; for you have hidden your face from us, and have made us melt in the hand of our iniquities (ESV Isaiah 64:6-7).

As it is written: "There is no one righteous, not even one; there is no one who understands, no one who seeks God. All have turned away, they have together become worthless; there is no one who does good, not even one." "Their throats are open graves; their tongues practice deceit." "The poison of vipers is on their lips." "Their mouths are full of cursing and bitterness." "Their feet are swift to shed blood; ruin and misery mark their ways, and the way of peace they do not know." "There is no fear of God before their eyes." (ESV Romans 3:10-18)

PSYCHOPATHY SURVIVAL GUIDE

Know what you are dealing with. This can be very difficult. All the reading in the world cannot immunize you from the devastating effects of psychopaths. Even experts are conned and bewildered by them. A good psychopath can play a concerto on anyone's heart strings.

Try not to be influenced by "props." It is not easy to get beyond the winning smile, the captivating body language, the fast talk of the typical psychopath, all of which blind us to his or her real intentions. Many people find it difficult to deal with the intense, "predatory state" of the psychopath. The fixated stare, is more about self-gratification and the exercise of power rather than simple interest or empathic caring.

Don't wear blinders. Enter new relationships with your eyes wide open. Like the rest of us, most psychopathic con artists and "love-thieves" initially hide their dark side by putting their "best foot forward." Cracks may soon begin to appear in the mask they wear, but once trapped in their web, it is difficult to escape financially and emotionally unscathed.

Keep your guard up in high-risk situations. Some situations are tailor-made for psychopaths: singles bars, ship cruises, foreign airports, etc. In each case, the potential victim is lonely, looking for a good time, excitement, or companionship, and there will usually be someone willing to oblige, for a hidden price.

Know yourself. Psychopaths are skilled at detecting and ruthlessly exploiting your weak spots. Your best defense is to understand what these spots are, and to be extremely wary of anyone who zeroes in on them (Hare, This Charming Psychopath, *Psychology Today*).

HELPFUL RESOURCES

BOOKS
- Without Conscience: The Disturbing World of the Psychopaths Among Us
- Snakes in Suits: When Psychopaths Go to Work
- Psychopathy: An Important Forensic Concept for the 21st Century (FBI LEB)
- The Anatomy of Evil
- The Sociopath Next Door
- Psychopath Free: Recovering from Emotionally Abusive Relationships with Narcissists, Sociopaths, & Other Toxic People
- Dangerous Instincts: Use an FBI Profiler's Tactics to Avoid Unsafe Situations
- In Sheep's Clothing: Understanding and Dealing with Manipulative People

ORGANIZATIONS
- Society for the Scientific Study of Psychopathy (SSSP)
- Aftermath: Surviving Psychopathy Foundation
- American Academy of Forensic Psychology (AAFP)

- American Academy of Forensic Sciences (AAFS)
- International Cultic Studies Association (ICSA)
- Safe Place Ministries (SPM)

WEBSITES
- "Without Conscience" (Robert Hare's Website)
- Psychopathy Awareness
- Psychopath Free
- FBI Victim Assistance

MINISTRY APPLICATIONS

The church has largely failed its families who have been manipulated and damaged by people with psychopathic and sociopathic traits. More church recovery ministries and parachurch ministries like Safe Place Ministries and Aftermath are needed to help families recover from abusive spouses, domestic partners, parents, and other relationships. Other applications include:

- Cult-proofing your church and your children.
- Implementing counter-cult recovery and outreach ministries.
- Addressing issues of cognitive and functional biblical illiteracy.
- Implementing a comprehensive apologetics curriculum.

CONCLUSIONS

- Psychopathy is the worst of the 10 personality disorders.
- Psychopaths and sociopaths are not the same.
- Psychopathy is misunderstood and generally disliked by the mental health community because it is not treatable.
- Most psychopaths are not serial killers.
- Subcriminal (white collar) psychopaths can be successful individuals having careers as entrepreneurs, politicians, CEOs, or other respectable positions.
- Diagnosis of psychopaths can only be done by trained clinicians.

- Forensic psychology (psychopathy) should be studied by Christians because this unique personality disorder cannot be defined by traditional humanistic mental health disciplines.
- Psychopaths are the worst of the worst but one does not need to be one to commit evil acts such as crimes of opportunity or passion.
- Psychopaths are predisposed but not predetermined to be evil.
- The ethical systems used by psychopaths are ethical egoism and consequentialism.
- Recent neuroscience studies on the brains of psychopaths indicates that the dysfunctional amygdala is different than non-psychopaths.
- Christians should develop an apologetics of human behavior that shows that negative aspects of the reality of evil in order to compliment Godly biblical teaching on good behavior.
- Christian should develop an apologetics of the depravity of human nature, ethics, and morals that includes clinical and forensic data to compliment biblical teaching.
- Christian should develop an apologetics of safety and security that trains people about red flags regarding dangerous human behavior and relationships.

"In his famous essay Thus Spake Zarathustra, Nietzsche created a powerful image relating to our task as human beings. We pass through the years of our lives like a tightrope walker perched precariously on his rope. "Man," as he put it, "is a rope stretched between animal and the superior man; the rope lies over the abyss." We can fall back to the animal level-or we can strive toward the goal of self-transcendence and moral superiority. I am a little uncomfortable with the "animal" image. It is only we humans, not our animal cousins, who are capable of evil, though people (referring to some evil act) are accustomed to say, "He behaved like an animal." Perhaps a more up-to-date analogy might be: We are a rope stretched between Bundy and the Buddha. And the abyss is the descent to the evil of Ted Bundy and his like, where all regard for the welfare of one's fellow man evaporates, leaving one capable of immeasurable cruelty and harm. Harm that shocks us. Evil." (Stone, TAE, 4527-4532).

QUESTIONS FOR DISCUSSION

1. Does a person need to be a psychopath or sociopath to be evil?

2. What is the ultimate evil?

3. Would you know a psychopath if you saw one?

4. Is it possible for ethical and moral dilemmas to be win-win for all parties? Why or why not?

5. Is it a flawed methodology to test psychopaths using consequentialist ethics? Why or why not?

6. Is moral evil worse than natural or metaphysical evil? Why or why not?

7. Should we educate people on the dangers of encountering psychopaths and sociopaths? Why or why not?

8. Are psychopaths and sociopaths predetermined to be evil? Why or why not?

9. Why doesn't God end all moral evil immediately?

10. What can churches and mental health organizations do to train and minister to people who have been damaged by psychopaths and sociopaths?

APPENDIX A: DR. STONE GRADATIONS OF EVIL SCALE

Killing in Self-Defense or Justified Homicide	
Category 1.	Justifiable homicide
Impulsive Murders in Persons without Psychopathic Features	
Category 2.	Jealous lovers, egocentric, immature people, committing crimes of passion
Category 3.	Willing companions of killers, impulse-ridden; some antisocial trait
Category 4.	Killing in self-defense, but extremely provocative toward the victim
Category 5.	Traumatized, desperate persons who kill relatives or others, yet have remorse
Category 6.	Impetuous, hotheaded murders, yet without marked psychopathic traits
Persons with a Few or No Psychopathic Traits; Murders of a More Severe Type	
Category 7.	Highly narcissistic persons, some with a psychotic core, who murder loved ones
Category 8.	Murders sparked by smoldering rage—resulting sometimes in mass murder
Psychopathic Features Marked; Murders Show Malice Aforethought	
Category 9.	Jealous lovers with strong psychopathic traits or full-blown psychopathy
Category 10.	Killers of people "in the way" (including witnesses); extreme egocentricity
Category 11.	Fully psychopathic killers of people "in the way"
Category 12.	Power-hungry psychopaths who murder when "cornered"
Category 13.	Inadequate, rageful psychopaths; some committing multiple murders
Category 14.	Ruthlessly self-centered psychopathic schemers
Spree or Multiple Murders; Psychopathy is Apparent	
Category 15.	Psychopathic, cold-blooded, spree or multiple murderers
Category 16.	Psychopathic persons committing multiple vicious acts (including murder)
Serial Killers, Torturers, Sadists	
Category 17.	Sexually perverse serial killers; killing is to hide evidence; no torture
Category 18.	Torture-murderers, though the torture element is not prolonged
Category 19.	Psychopaths driven to terrorism, subjugation, rape, etc. short of murder
Category 20.	Torture-murderers but in persons with distinct psychosis (such as schizophrenia)
Category 21.	Psychopaths committing extreme torture but not known to have killed
Category 22.	Psychopathic torture-murders with torture as their primary motive. The motive need not always be sexual.
Source: Stone, TAE, 523.	

Appendix B: Ezekiel 18

- **1** The word of the LORD came to me: **2** "What do you people mean by quoting this proverb about the land of Israel: " 'The fathers eat sour grapes, and the children's teeth are set on edge'? **3** "As surely as I live, declares the Sovereign LORD, you will no longer quote this proverb in Israel. **4** For every living soul belongs to me, the father as well as the son--both alike belong to me. The soul who sins is the one who will die. **5** "Suppose there is a righteous man who does what is just and right. **6** He does not eat at the mountain shrines or look to the idols of the house of Israel. He does not defile his neighbor's wife or lie with a woman during her period. **7** He does not oppress anyone but returns what he took in pledge for a loan. He does not commit robbery but gives his food to the hungry and provides clothing for the naked. **8** He does not lend at usury or take excessive interest. He withholds his hand from doing wrong and judges fairly between man and man.

- **9** He follows my decrees and faithfully keeps my laws. That man is righteous; he will surely live, declares the Sovereign LORD. **10** "Suppose he has a violent son, who sheds blood or does any of these other things **11** (though the father has done none of them): "He eats at the mountain shrines. He defiles his neighbor's wife. **12** He oppresses the poor and needy. He commits robbery. He does not return what he took in pledge. He looks to the idols. He does detestable things. **13** He lends at usury and takes excessive interest. Will such a man live? He will not! Because he has done all these detestable things, he will surely be put to death and his blood will be on his own head. **14** "But suppose this son has a son who sees all the sins his father commits, and though he sees them, he does not do such things: **15** "He does not eat at the mountain shrines or look to the idols of the house of Israel. He does not defile his neighbor's wife. **16** He does not oppress anyone or require a pledge for a loan. He does not commit robbery but gives his food to the hungry and provides clothing for the naked.

- **17** He withholds his hand from sin and takes no usury or excessive interest. He keeps my laws and follows my decrees. He will not die for his father's sin; he will surely live. **18** But his father will die for his own sin, because he practiced extortion, robbed his brother and did what was wrong among his people. **19** "Yet you ask, 'Why does the son not share the guilt of his father?' Since the son has done what is just and right and has been careful to keep all my decrees, he will surely live. **20** The soul who sins is the one who will die. The son will not share the guilt of the father, nor will the father share the guilt of the son. The righteousness of the righteous man will be credited to him, and the wickedness of the wicked will be charged against him. **21** "But if a wicked man turns away from all the sins he has committed and keeps all my decrees and does what is just and right, he will surely live; he will not die. **22** None of the offenses he has committed will be remembered against him. Because of the righteous things he has done, he will live. **23** Do I take any pleasure in the death of the wicked? declares the Sovereign LORD. Rather, am I not pleased when they turn from their ways and live?
- **24** "But if a righteous man turns from his righteousness and commits sin and does the same detestable things the wicked man does, will he live? None of the righteous things he has done will be remembered. Because of the unfaithfulness he is guilty of and because of the sins he has committed, he will die. **25** "Yet you say, 'The way of the Lord is not just.' Hear, O house of Israel: Is my way unjust? Is it not your ways that are unjust? **26** If a righteous man turns from his righteousness and commits sin, he will die for it; because of the sin he has committed he will die. **27** But if a wicked man turns away from the wickedness he has committed and does what is just and right, he will save his life. **28** Because he considers all the offenses he has committed and turns away from them, he will surely live; he will not die. **29** Yet the house of Israel says, 'The way of the Lord is not just.' Are my ways unjust, O house of Israel? Is it not your ways that are unjust? **30** "Therefore, O house of Israel, I will judge you,

each one according to his ways, declares the Sovereign LORD. Repent! Turn away from all your offenses; then sin will not be your downfall. **31** Rid yourselves of all the offenses you have committed and get a new heart and a new spirit. Why will you die, O house of Israel? **32** For I take no pleasure in the death of anyone, declares the Sovereign LORD. Repent and live!

APPENDIX C: JOHN AND BILL

- John and Bill had been close friends for many years. They were next-door neighbors in the same small Ohio town and attended the same Christian church. Both were good students during high school.

- They were therefore pleased when both were admitted to the same college. As part of their orientation, John and Bill signed a pledge not to cheat and to report anyone who did.

- The semester started well, with both young men taking premed courses with the hope of becoming doctors and starting a practice together.

- Their goal was to start a free clinic to serve the working poor. But Bill ran into difficulty after several weeks.

- First, his father suffered a severe heart attack, and then his girlfriend indicated that she no longer wanted to continue their long-distance relationship.

- John and Bill were in organic chemistry together, a course that was critical for getting into medical school.

- Bill was not well prepared for the midterm, which counted for half their grade and was graded on a curve, based on the outcomes of all the students in the class.

- As the exam ended and they walked out of the classroom, Bill breathed a sigh of relief. "Well," he said, "I think I did OK." "Great," replied John. "I think I did pretty well, too."

- Later that night, after a few beers, Bill said to John, "Can I tell you something in confidence?" "Sure," said John. Bill proceeded to tell his good friend that he had taken notes to the exam and had used them for his answers.

- John was shocked because he had always known Bill to be honest and trustworthy. He told Bill that he should go to Professor Williams and admit what he did.

- Bill replied that he would never cheat again, but that he wouldn't turn himself in because he "knew" that other students were cheating, too.

- The next day, John was called into Professor Williams's office. The professor said, "I know that you are good friends with Bill. I suspect him of cheating on the midterm. He has denied it. Do you know anything about it?" (Fedler, *ECE*, 210-221)

APPENDIX D: DR. LONNIE ATHENS

- When considering origins of violent criminal actions, the sociological explanations favored by many that crime is an outgrowth of poverty and bad environment is simplistic and misleading.
- Sociologists claim that inherited factors may have paved the way for the ensuing brutality to have its devastating effects.
- Consider the case of Dr. Lonnie Athens who was consistently brutalized his parents in his formative years before passing into the stage of virulency.
- Dr. Athens's own life gives the lie to his one-sided theory. He himself had been brutalized by his father in ways that would be sickening to describe here.
- Yet he did not go on to become a violent (let alone virulent or evil) criminal. How can this be?
- The safest assumption is that Dr. Athens was dealt some genetic high cards that allowed him to endure his father's tortures without succumbing to a life of vengeance and criminality, becoming instead an eminent sociologist with some special insights into the lives of violent felons (Stone, TAE, 4325-4331).

APPENDIX E: SANFORD CLARK

- Consider the similar case of "good seed" Sanford Clark, the half-brother of Gordon Northcott.
- When Sanford was 13, he was taken by his much older brother (whom he was raised by their mother to believe was his uncle) to a California chicken ranch.
- There he was raped and beaten regularly by Gordon and forced at gunpoint to participate in the rape-murders of 20 Mexican boys.
- It was Sanford's job to flay the victims, crush their skulls, and dispose of their remains.
- After 2 years of this enslavement, he was able to escape and give evidence against Northcott, who was hanged two years later in 1930.
- After overcoming immense psychological traumas, Sanford made a good recovery.
- He married and adopted 2 boys, afraid to taint any children he might have of his own (there were other violent and abusive relatives besides his half-brother).
- Sanford Clark was able to lead an exemplary life-for reasons as mysterious as why Athens's father and Clark's brother were so consistently evil (Stone, TAE, 4331-4336).

APPENDIX F: JOSEPH DUNCAN

- Note the case of serial killer Joseph Duncan. After a long series of rapes and murders of young boys, he was released as a "sex offender" (rather than as a "sex predator") thanks to a lax prison system.
- Reoffending shortly afterward (sexually groping a six-year-old boy), he manipulated a friend into putting up bail money-and then skipped bail.
- A month later, Duncan kidnapped a boy and a girl, after killing their mother, brother, and the mother's fiancé.
- Taking them from Idaho to Montana, he raped and tortured them for two months, making a video of the torture, and finally killing the nine-year-old boy.
- The sister managed to escape further abuse when Duncan was apprehended with her while in a convenience store.
- Convicting Duncan in 2008 in Idaho, the jury recommended the death penalty.
- Duncan meets criteria for Category 22, the highest on Dr. Stone's scale of evil.
- Duncan came from a good home, was not abused, was very bright, and did not show the triad-though he did wet the bed until age thirteen.
- The factors behind his psychopathy seem attributable more to nature than to nurture. But it was the inappropriate release from prison that allowed this sex offender to continue their violent careers-their violence actually escalated in the post-release years (Stone, TAE, 4437-4441).

Appendix G: Drazen Erdomovic

- Note the case of 24-year-old Drazen Erdomovic, a half-Serb, half-Croat soldier transported in mid-July with his unit in 1995 to Srebrenica, not knowing what his mission was.
- His commander, Brano Gojkovic, soon made his mission clear: he was to join with his mates in shooting to death some 1200 Muslim civilians, men and boys, who had been bused there for the purpose.
- As Drakulic tells the story, Drazen had no taste for this sort of thing. When he expressed his disinclination to take part in the massacre, his mates mocked him. He was after all only a half-Serb in their eyes: not someone they could readily trust.
- His commander then told him: "If you don't want to do it, walk over there and stand with the prisoners so we can shoot you too. Give me your machine gun."
- Now Drazen is given the choice between a good and an evil. He could stand on moral high ground-and die. Or he could kill some innocent men and boys-and live, perhaps to tell the world of the still greater evil into which he was forced by his commander, who obeyed an even worse commander, General Mladic, who gleefully carried out the orders of Dr. Karadzic, who-ignoring the Hippocratic Oath ("First, do no harm")-happily obeyed the genocidal edict of President Slobodan Milosevic.
- Drazen chose life-for himself, which meant the deaths of the 60 people he spent a quarter-hour shooting.
- He did tell the story, and because his story was believable, his sentence at court was reduced from 10 years to 5.
- Was it better that Drazen live to let the world know what happened on that killing field? Or would it have been better if he (and all the men compelled to take part in the massacre) died, leaving the truly evil and guilty commanders and generals and presidents to live out their lives unsuspected and unpunished?
- Because Drazen had a conscience, he lives on as a spiritually broken man. And Mladic and Karadzic live on, too-contented and unrepentant.

- In the young soldier's place, what would I have done? What would you have done? I ask this only as a rhetorical question. If we are honest, we cannot say what we would have done (Stone, TAE, 4225-4238).

REFERENCES

- Babiak, Paul; Hare, Robert D. (2009-10-13). *Snakes in Suits: When Psychopaths Go to Work*. HarperCollins. Kindle Edition.
- Birch, "Psychopathy: Is It In Their Eyes?" Psychopaths & Love. http://psychopathsandlove.com/psychopathy-and-the-eyes/.
- Columbia Business School. "Antisocial personality traits predict utilitarian responses to moral dilemmas." *ScienceDaily*. www.sciencedaily.com/releases/2011/09/110930153042.htm.
- Fedler, Kyle D. *Exploring Christian Ethics: Biblical Foundations for Morality*. Louisville: Westminster John Knox Press, 2006. Kindle Edition.
- Gleichgerrcht E, Young L (2013). "Low Levels of Empathic Concern Predict Utilitarian Moral Judgment." *PLoS ONE* 8(4): e60418. doi:10.1371/journal.pone.0060418.
- Hare, Robert D. Hare Psychopathy Checklist-Revised, 2nd ed. Toronto, ON: Multi-Health Systems, 2003.
- _____. "This Charming Psychopath: How to spot social predators before they attack." *Psychology Today*. http://www.psychologytoday.com/articles/199401/charming-psychopath.
- _____. Without Conscience: The Disturbing World of the Psychopaths Among Us. New York: The Guilford Press, 1993. Kindle edition.
- "Hare Psychopathy Checklist." Encyclopedia of Mental Disorders. http://www.minddisorders.com/Flu-Inv/Hare-Psychopathy-Checklist.html#ixzz2pggmBRxq.
- Koenigs, Michael, et. al. "Utilitarian moral judgment in psychopathy." SCAN (2012) 7, 708-714: doi:10.1093/scan/nsr048.
- Myers, Wade C., Erik Gooch and J. Reid Meloy. "The Role of Psychopathy and Sexuality in a Female Serial Killer." *J Forensic Sci 50 (3)*. May 2005.
- Pujols, J., et. al. "Breakdown in the brain network subserving moral judgment in criminal psychopathy." SCAN (2012) 7,917-923: doi:10.1093/scan/nsr075.

- Seabrook, John. *Suffering Souls: The search for the roots of psychopathy.* November 10, 2008. www.newyorker.com/reporting/2008/11/10/081110fa_fact_seabrook? (accessed October 23, 2013).
- Stone, Michael H. *The Anatomy of Evil.* New York: Prometheus Books, 2009. Kindle edition.